Student
DISCUSSION GUIDE

to

The Hobbit

By Ann Maouyo

JHU Talent Development Secondary
Center for Social Organization of Schools
Johns Hopkins University
Baltimore

Discussion Guide #1

Chapters 1–3

Vocabulary List A

porthole (p. 1)
pantries (p. 1)
wardrobes (p. 1)
blundering (p. 2)
fabulous (p. 2)
absurd (p. 2)
discreetly (p. 3)
luxurious (p. 3)
immovably (p. 3)
numerous (p. 3)
*prosperous (p. 3)
*extraordinary (p. 3)
unsuspecting (p. 4)
immense (p. 4)
laburnums (p. 5)
prosy (p. 5)
profitable (p. 6)
scuttled (p. 6)
flustered (adj., p. 6)
cloak (p. 7)
spade (n., p. 8)
throng (n., p. 8)
depredations (p. 9)
ale (p. 9)
porter (p. 9)

scones (p. 9)
immensely (p. 10)
haughty (p. 10)
larders (p. 11)
wretched (p. 11)
thereupon (p. 11)
tread (v., p. 12)
crocks (p. 12)
viols (p. 13)
yore (p. 14)
hoard (p. 14)
wrought (p. 14)
hilt (p. 14)
goblets (p. 14)
ire (p. 14)
frail (p. 14)
doom (p. 15)
*grim (p. 15)
cunning (n., p. 15)
plundering (adj., p. 15)
kindling (v., p. 15)
apologetically (p. 16)
conspirator (p. 16)
*audacious (p. 16)
*ingenious (p. 16)
estimable (p. 16)

descendant (p. 17)
reviving (p. 17)
drawing-room (p. 17)
parlor (p. 17)
expedition (p. 18)
scowled (p. 19)
parchment (p. 19)
devouring (p. 20)
intricate (p. 20)
alters (p. 20)
scarce (p. 21)
legendary (p. 21)
obstinately (p. 22)
*prudent (p. 22)
remuneration (p. 22)
reverence (p. 22)
mortal (p. 22)
smiths (p. 22)
apprentices (p. 22)
notion (p. 23)
market value (p. 23)
routed (p. 23)
singed (adj., p. 24)
heir (p. 24)
stowed (p. 26)

Special Glossary

time out of mind - a very long time; as long as anyone can remember

braces - suspenders

lads and lasses - *(Old English and Scottish)* young men and women

tea - *(British)* a light meal taken around 4 p.m.

queer - odd; unusual

collect my wits - calm down; gather my thoughts; think calmly about something

flummoxed - *(old slang)* confused; bewildered

fells - barren, empty hillsides

delves - digs

dale - a valley

runes - mysterious characters of an ancient alphabet

curious - here, odd; strange; unusual

wards - ridges and notches in a key

 The Writer's Craft

Exposition and Conflict

The **plot**, or action in a story, includes several basic elements:

1) The **exposition**;
2) The **conflict** (problems to be solved);
3) The **climax** or high point of the action; and
4) The **denouement** or resolution of the problems.

continued on page 3

In the first part, the exposition, the author "sets the scene." We learn about the characters and the setting—the time and place in which the action occurs. Perhaps we learn something of the background of the story. We might begin to suspect what problems the characters will have to face— in other words, what the conflict is going to be.

As you read the first chapter of *The Hobbit,* watch for information about the main characters, their background and their personalities. Also see how much you can learn about the setting of the story.

DISCUSSION QUESTIONS AND ACTIVITIES

Section I. Read chapter 1. Discuss your responses to the questions and activities with a classmate. Then write your answers independently.

1. **The author insists on the fact that there are two sides to Bilbo's personality. These two sides correspond to the two sides of his family: the Tooks and the Bagginses. In the chart below, show the difference between the Took side and the Baggins side of Bilbo. List adjectives that might be used to describe each side, as well as remarks and reactions that are typical of each side.**

	Bilbo's Baggins Side	Bilbo's Took Side
Adjectives describing each side		
Remarks and reactions typical of each side		

2. **What do we learn about Gandalf in this first chapter? What is his relationship with the dwarves?**

_____

_____

_____

_____

_____

_____

3. **What do we learn about the dwarves, their origins, and their background? What impression do we have of Thorin Oakenshield, their leader?**

_____

_____

_____

_____

_____

_____

4. **What do we learn from this chapter about the *conflict* of the story? What is Bilbo's role expected to be? What do you think Gandalf means when he describes Bilbo as a "burglar"?**

_____

_____

_____

_____

_____

_____

_____

5. **What is the *setting* of the first chapter? Contrast the *mood* or feeling this setting gives you, with the hints that we are given about the setting of the chapters to come.**

_____

_____

_____

_____

_____

_____

_____

Make A
Prediction:

**What will Bilbo find
when he wakes up
the next morning?**

Vocabulary List B

*outlandish (p. 28)
mantelpiece (p. 29)
defrayed (p. 29)
esteemed (adj., p. 29)
repose (n., p. 29)
requisite (p. 29)
paraphernalia (p. 30)
laden (p. 30)
inhabited (p. 31)
ambling (p. 31)
steadily (p. 31)
dreary (p. 31)
bolted (v., p. 33)
reflecting (p. 33)
*inquisitive (p. 33)
canny (p. 34)
cavalcade (p. 34)
primly (p. 34)
mutton (p. 34)
trolls (n., p. 35)

sheltered (adj., p. 35)
purloined (p. 36)
throttled (p. 36)
startled (p. 36)
lout (p. 37)
applicable (p. 38)
detest (p. 38)
mince (p. 39)
bickering (p. 41)
suffocated (p. 41)
incantations (p. 42)
scabbards (p. 43)
*provisions (p. 43)
scanty (p. 43)
embers (p. 43)
replenishing (p. 44)
waylaid (p. 44)
forded (p. 45)
vast (p. 46)

heather (p. 46)
dwelling (n., p. 46)
gullies (p. 47)
ravines (p. 47)
bogs (n., p. 47)
drowsy (p. 48)
reeking (p. 48)
straying (p. 49)
folly (p. 49)
parapet (p. 50)
*venerable (p. 51)
lair (p. 52)
whence (p. 52)
remnants (p. 52)
pondered (p. 52)
cleave (p. 52)
crescent (p. 53)
vexed (adj., p. 53)
thrush (p. 53)
threshold (p. 53)

Special Glossary

copped - *(British regional slang)* grabbed; stolen

slow in the uptake - slow to understand; not very smart

row - *(British*; pronounce to rhyme with "cow") a heated quarrel or fight

caught unawares - taken by surprise

in the nick of time - just in time

bannocks - *(Scottish)* thick, flat pancakes made of oatmeal or barley meal

midsummer's eve - the eve of the summer solstice, around June 20

 The Writer's Craft

Fantasy

Fantasy is a type of fiction based on pure imagination. The action may depend on magical or supernatural elements. It differs in this way from realistic fiction, in which the stories are true to life and seem as if they could have happened, even though they actually did not. **Fairy tales** and **folk tales** are traditional types of fantasy that usually have fairly simple story lines and **flat characters**: the good characters are all good and the evil characters are completely evil.

However, some writers create works of fantasy by imagining an entire world that is in some ways like our own world, and in some ways very different. For example, writers of **science fiction** (another type of fantasy) often imagine a time in the distant future, either on Earth or on another planet entirely. Their imaginary worlds usually depend, not on magic or the supernatural, but on amazing imagined advances in science and technology.

continued on page 8

J.R.R. Tolkien's world, on the other hand, looks back to the distant past. In some ways it is similar to old stories called **romances** that have been popular since the Middle Ages. No, not necessarily love stories (although sometimes the old-fashioned romances did include love stories). The romances were fantastic adventure stories of heroic deeds. The most famous example is the story of King Arthur and the Knights of the Round Table.

In some ways, though, Tolkien's world is different from that of the romances. Whether his characters are hobbits or dwarves or other imaginary creatures, their personalities are surprisingly similar to those of real, ordinary people: both good and bad, brave and fearful, selfish and noble. Many scholars consider Tolkien the founder of the modern genre of fantasy. Other modern fantasy writers include C.S. Lewis, Mary Norton, Lloyd Alexander, and Susan Cooper.

As you read the next two chapters, watch for ways that Bilbo's world is both similar to, and different from, the real world.

DISCUSSION QUESTIONS AND ACTIVITIES

Section II. Read chapters 2 and 3. Discuss your responses to the questions and activities with a classmate. Then write your answers independently.

1. **What surprises are waiting for Bilbo when he gets up? How does he feel about the situation? Read carefully the note that Thorin left for Bilbo on the mantelpiece. If you were in Bilbo's place, how would you feel after reading this message?**

_____

_____

_____

_____

_____

_____

2. **How does the countryside change after the first few weeks of travel? What effect does the bad weather have on the travelers' attitudes and behavior toward one another?**

_____

_____

_____

_____

_____

_____

_____

3. **Why does Bilbo try to pick the troll's pocket? How does his handling of this situation show his lack of experience as a "burglar"?**

_____

_____

_____

_____

_____

_____

4. **How are Bilbo and the dwarves rescued from the trolls? What does this incident show us about Gandalf and his powers?**

_____

_____

_____

_____

_____

_____

5. **Why are the travelers anxious to reach Rivendell? What important information do they learn there, both about the swords they took from the trolls' cave and about Thorin's map?**

_____

_____

_____

_____

_____

_____

_____

Make A
Prediction:

**What dangers will
Bilbo and the
dwarves face in the
Misty Mountains?**

  Literature-Related Writing

1. How do you think the other hobbits reacted to Bilbo's sudden disappearance? Write an imaginary **news article** for the "Hobbiton Gazette." Describe the mysterious circumstances surrounding his departure and report on the community's reaction.

2. Create an imaginary **travel brochure** inviting tourists to visit Tolkien's Middle Earth. Based on what you have learned so far, describe accommodations and some of the interesting attractions, as well as important warnings for travelers' safety and well being during their visit. Use your imagination to think of a creative means of transportation to take your customers to Middle Earth!

3. Imagine a fantasy world of your own. In a brief **essay** of three to five paragraphs, describe your world and the creatures that inhabit it. Before you begin to write, think about the following questions: Is it a world similar to Earth, or is it found on a different type of planet? Is it a _futuristic_ (science fiction) type of world, or an ancient (mythological) one? What does it look like? Is it made up of cities or countryside? Is it a good place, a bad place, or a little of both? What types of beings or intelligent life are found there? What place (if any) do magic and/or technology have in this world? What possible _conflicts_ might arise in this world? (Save your essay—you may need it for future Literature-Related Writing activities.)

Extension Activities

1. With one or more other students, act out a scene from chapter 1.

2. Draw portraits of Bilbo, Gandalf, and Thorin Oakenshield, based on the descriptions found in the book.

3. Illustrate a scene of your choice from these chapters. Be sure to portray both the setting and the characters in a way that is consistent with the description found in the book.

4. Make a cartoon strip of the travelers' encounter with the trolls.

Discussion Guide #2

Chapters 4–6

Vocabulary List A

passes (n., p. 55)	hospitable (p. 63)	slays (p. 77)
deceptions (p. 55)	gnashed (p. 64)	antiquity (p. 79)
*infested (adj., p. 55)	breeches (p. 69)	galled (p. 81)
boulders (p. 55)	*subterranean (p. 70)	*groping (adj., p. 83)
drenched (p. 57)	unbeknown (p. 71)	shambling (v., p. 85)
passage (p. 59)	dangling (p. 71)	*menacingly (p. 86)
shirk (p. 61)	prowling (p. 71)	*incline (n., p. 87)
quaff (p. 61)	lurking (p. 71)	ventured (p. 88)
alliances (p. 62)	gnaws (p. 77)	giddy (p. 89)

Special Glossary

I'll warrant - *(slang)* I'll bet; I'm quite sure

chestnuts - *(idiom)* very old, stale, well-known jokes or riddles

poser - a very difficult question or riddle

at a pinch - *(idiom; usually* "in a pinch"*)* in an emergency; under pressure

blindman's buff - *(usually* "blindman's bluff"*)* a game in which one player is blindfolded

The Writer's Craft

Onomatopoeia

Onomatopoeia is a term used to describe words that actually sound like the action that they describe—words like "crunch," "dribble," or "pop." Onomatopoeic words make us feel as if we are right in the middle of the story. Tolkien likes to use onomatopoeic words, especially in action scenes. As you read the next two chapters, notice the onomatopoeic words. How do the words used to describe the encounter with the goblins differ from those used in the description of that odd creature Gollum? How do these words contribute to our impressions of these very different characters?

Foreshadowing

Foreshadowing in literature means giving clues about events that are going to happen later on in the story. Chapter 4 contains many hints about what is going to happen, well before it *does* happen. What are these hints? How do you feel when you come across hints like these as you are reading?

DISCUSSION QUESTIONS AND ACTIVITIES

Section I. Read chapters 4 and 5. Discuss your responses to the questions and activities with a classmate. Then write your answers independently.

1. **List the hints that *foreshadow* the goblins' surprise attack well before it occurs.**

    _____

    _____

    _____

    _____

    _____

    _____

    _____

2. **Use the Venn diagram below to show the similarities and differences between dwarves and goblins.**

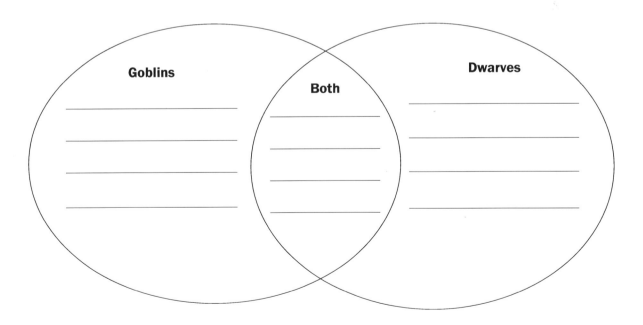

3. **Chapter 4 contains a lot of "good news" and "bad news" for Bilbo and the dwarves. Use the sequence chart below to show their ups and downs.**

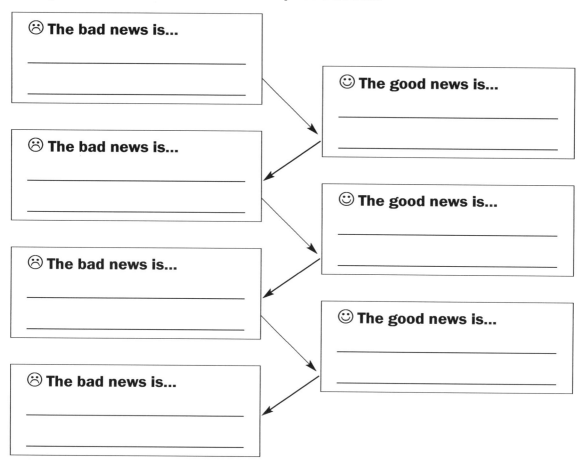

4. **What do we learn about Gollum's background, way of life, and character in chapter 5? Why does he suggest playing a riddle game with Bilbo?**

_____

_____

_____

_____

_____

_____

5. **What is Gollum's plan when he returns to his island? What goes wrong? Why do you think the narrator says that finding the ring was "a turning point" in Bilbo's career?**

_____

_____

_____

_____

_____

_____

_____

Make A
Prediction:

Will Bilbo be able to find Gandalf and the dwarves again?

Vocabulary List B

abominable (p. 91)
*onslaught (p. 97)
bracken (p. 97)
fronds (p. 97)
*intervals (p. 99)
boughs (p. 99)
glade (p. 99)
clambered (p. 100)

clamor (n., p. 100)
commotion (p. 102)
pinnacle (p. 103)
glint (n., p. 103)
cowardly (p. 103)
lofty (p. 104)
afoot (p. 104)
fiery (p. 105)
borne (p. 107)

*tumult (p. 107)
spikes (n., p. 107)
bids (v., p. 108)
*precipice (p. 108)
yew (p. 109)
obliged (adj., p. 109)
*famished (p. 109)
contentedly (p. 110)

Glossary of Special Terms

dells - small glens or hollows in the ground

benighted - caught by nightfall

eyrie - (alternate spelling of "aerie") the nest of an eagle or other bird of prey

The Writer's Craft

Suspense

In the first section of this Partner Discussion Guide, you observed the many hints that foreshadowed something terrible happening to Bilbo and the dwarves. When you first read those hints, you probably wondered, "What is it? What will happen next?"

That "what will happen next" feeling is called **suspense**. Writers create suspense in many ways. Foreshadowing is one of them. Another way of creating suspense is to portray frightening settings and desperate situations so that the reader wonders how the characters will escape—*if* they do escape. Suspense is also created when characters find themselves going back and forth between "good news" and "bad news," as we observed in chapter 4. As you read the next chapter, notice how the writer captures our attention and creates suspense about what will happen to Bilbo and his companions.

DISCUSSION QUESTIONS AND ACTIVITIES

Section II. Read chapter 6. Discuss your responses to the questions and activities with a class-mate. Then write your answers independently.

1. **What does Bilbo realize when he sees that the sun is setting *behind* the mountain? What else does he learn from listening to the dwarves' discussions with Gandalf?**

_____

_____

_____

_____

_____

_____

2. **What does Bilbo leave out of the story when he tells the dwarves what happened to him? Why do you think he leaves this out? Discuss whether or not you think this is a good decision on Bilbo's part.**

_____

_____

_____

_____

_____

_____

3. **Why is the clearing place in the forest a very bad place for the travelers to spend the night? Describe Gandalf's strategy for keeping the wolves away, and explain how the goblins turn it against the travelers.**

_____

_____

_____

_____

_____

_____

_____

4. **Explain how the travelers are rescued. Why does Bilbo find that the rescue itself is a frightening experience?**

_____

_____

_____

_____

_____

_____

_____

5. **Describe Bilbo's dream as he sleeps in the eagle's nest. What do you think this dream might mean?**

_____

_____

_____

_____

_____

_____

_____

Make A
Prediction:

Where will the eagles take the travelers after their night's sleep?

Literature-Related Writing

1. Write an imaginary State Department **memorandum** to warn travelers planning a trip to the Misty Mountains about the dangers they may encounter. Also suggest precautions they should take to protect themselves.

2. Write a **poem** about the travelers' encounter with the wolves and their rescue by the Lord of the Eagles and his companions. Use **onomatopoeia** in your poem. It does not have to contain rhyme.

3. Use the description of an imaginary world you wrote for Partner Discussion Guide #1. Begin to write a **story** about some of the creatures in your world. Use some of the techniques we have observed in _The Hobbit_ to create **suspense** and keep your readers on the edge of their seats. Don't finish your story just yet; try to leave the reader in suspense.

Extension Activities

1. With another student, tape record Bilbo's meeting with Gollum as a *radio play* (sound only). Don't forget to include appropriate sound effects, such as splashing water or footsteps. Play your recording for your class to enjoy.

2. Illustrate a scene from this section.

3. Do some research on real-life eagles (you may choose one particular species of eagle if you like). Share what you learn with your class.

Discussion Guide #3

Chapters 7 - 8

Vocabulary List A

plight (p. 113)   sleek (p. 117)   *wholesome (p. 131)
pleading (p. 114)   *intently (p. 117)   steeds (p. 132)
*appalling (p. 114)   tunic (p. 117)   scour (p. 133)
humored (p. 114)   gruffly (p. 117)   eaves (p. 134)
furrier (p. 114)   unimpeachable (p. 118)   pressing (adj., p. 135)
*perish (p. 115)   ram (n., p. 124)   wearisome (p. 136)
plodded (p. 116)   perils (p. 125)   *dismay (p. 138)
drones (p. 116)   vengeance (p. 130)   plunged (p. 138)

Special Glossary

in vain - unsuccessfully

conies - *(archaic)* a type of small rabbits; also, rabbit furs

tippets - long scarves made of fur

muffs - cylinders of fur used to keep the hands warm

trestles - rough tables made of boards laid across two pairs of spreading legs

mead - an alcoholic beverage made of fermented honey and water

The Writer's Craft

Complications

As we have seen, the main **conflict** in *The Hobbit* is Bilbo and the dwarves' struggle to reach the Mountain where they will face the terrible dragon Smaug. However, they have already faced many other problems and dangers along the way: trolls, goblins, Gollum, and wolves. These secondary problems are called **complications.** A complication is any new problem that makes the heroes', or **protagonists'**, situation even more complicated.

So far, different **antagonists** (or "bad guys") have caused most of the complications that Bilbo and the dwarves have faced. The next chapter, however, introduces a different type of complication. What is it? How do you think Bilbo and the dwarves will handle it?

DISCUSSION QUESTIONS AND ACTIVITIES

Section I. Read chapter 7. Discuss your responses to the questions and activities with a classmate. Then write your answers independently.

1. **What discouraging news does Gandalf give Bilbo and the dwarves when they arrive at the Carrock? How do they respond?**

2. **What kind of person is Beorn? Why does Gandalf warn Bilbo never to speak of anything having to do with furs while he is in Beorn's territory? Why does Gandalf have the dwarves arrive at Beorn's house by twos, at intervals spaced five minutes apart?**

_____

_____

_____

_____

_____

_____

3. **Compare and contrast Beorn's concerns with those of the dwarves. Why does Gandalf warn the travelers they must not go outside Beorn's house at night? Why does Beorn travel to the Misty Mountains the day after their arrival?**

_____

_____

_____

_____

_____

_____

4. **What assistance does Beorn offer the travelers for the next stage of their journey? What important advice does he give them?**

_____

_____

_____

_____

_____

_____

5. **Describe the dwarves' feelings when they reach Mirkwood. List reasons why they feel this way.**

_____

_____

_____

_____

_____

_____

Make A
Prediction:

**What will happen to
Bilbo and the
dwarves in the shad-
ows of Mirkwood?**

Vocabulary List B

lichen (p. 139)
undergrowth (p. 139)
bulbous (p. 141)
twilight (p. 146)
disquieting (p. 146)
eerie (p. 146)
trudge (p. 147)

flung (p. 148)
felled (adj., p. 151)
*consult (p. 151)
roused (p. 151)
mirth (p. 153)
evidently (p. 154)
*stealthily (p. 156)
wager (v., p. 156)

snares (n., p. 158)
*infuriate (p. 158)
astonishment (p. 163)
prey (n., p. 164)
*wary (p. 166)
tilling (p. 168)
*consequently (p. 168)

Special Glossary

tuppence - *(British)* two pennies; to "not care tuppence" means not to care at all

short commons - *(British)* short rations; not enough food for them to eat well

attercop - *(Old English)* word meaning "spider"

tomnoddy - *(British*; a seldom-used word) a foolish or stupid person

lob - (*Old English)* another word meaning "spider"

Faerie - a mythical land of magical beings

gloaming - *(Middle English and Scottish dialect)* dusk; twilight

 The Writer's Craft

Irony

Irony is a term used to describe a situation in which what really happens is very different from what was expected or what seemed to be happening. One common type of irony is **situational irony.** In situational irony, the reality of a situation turns out to be very different from what is expected or intended. Suppose you gave an old jacket that you considered worthless to a thrift store, not realizing that you had left a fifty-dollar bill in the pocket. This would certainly be situational irony.

As this example shows, situational irony can often be bitter or frustrating. In this section of *The Hobbit*, the dwarves send Bilbo to the top of a tree to see how much farther they must walk through the evil forest. What is ironic about what happens next? What is ironic about later events in this chapter?

DISCUSSION QUESTIONS AND ACTIVITIES

Section II. Read chapter 8. Discuss your responses to the questions and activities with a classmate. Then write your answers independently.

1. **List some of the hardships the travelers face as they make their way through Mirkwood. What unfortunate accident occurs as they cross the stream? How does it make their journey even more difficult?**

_____

_____

_____

_____

_____

_____

2. **Why do the dwarves send Bilbo up into a tree? What is the result of his report, and why is this _ironic_?**

_____

_____

_____

_____

_____

_____

_____

3. **On one side of the T-chart below, tell why the travelers want to stay on the path rather than follow the twinkling lights. On the other side, list reasons in favor of following the lights. What do they finally decide, and what is the result?**

Reason(s) For Staying on the Path	Reason(s) For Following the Lights

4. **How does Bilbo use personal qualities and skills as well as magical objects to rescue the party from the giant spiders? How does this incident change the dwarves' opinion of Bilbo, as well as Bilbo's feelings about himself?**

5. **Describe the relationship between the elves and the dwarves. Why does Thorin refuse to tell the elf-king why he and the other dwarves were in the forest? What is the result?**

_____

_____

_____

_____

_____

_____

_____

Make A
Prediction:

**Will Thorin escape from the elves' dungeon?
What will become of Bilbo and the other dwarves now that Thorin is also gone?**

Literature-Related Writing

1. Have you ever faced a difficult or challenging situation and learned that you had abilities or skills that you never suspected? Write a **personal narrative** about your experience. Describe the challenge you faced, how you overcame it, and what you learned about yourself.

2. Write a **song** or **poem** about one of the adventures recounted in these chapters.

3. Continue working on your story about your own imaginary world. Introduce some **complications** to the plot. You may wish to use **irony** as well. Don't finish your story yet, however—keep your readers in suspense a little longer!

Extension Activities

1. Create a model or diorama of Beorn's home.

2. Draw an illustration for a scene from this section.

3. Create a detailed map of the travelers' route in this section.

Discussion Guide #4

Chapters 9–12

Vocabulary List A

halt (v., p. 170)	jutting (adj., p. 185)	draggled (p. 194)
hewn (adj. p. 171)	dainties (p. 185)	solemnities (p. 194)
realm (p. 172)	suppressed (adj., p. 186)	comrades (p. 195)
*nimble (p. 173)	isles (p. 188)	quays (p. 195)
misfortunes (p. 174)	upkeep (p. 189)	vagabond (adj., p. 195)
quest (p. 174)	*attribute (v., p. 189)	molesting (p. 195)
ransom (v., p. 174)	alluding (p. 189)	hinder (p. 195)
watercourse (p. 175)	ominous (p. 189)	enmity (p. 196)
trapdoors (p.175)	receded (p. 190)	obscurest (p. 197)
*potent (p. 177)	shingles (p. 190)	pampered (p. 197)
heady (p. 177)	promontory (p. 190)	regained (p. 198)
vintage (p. 177)	drought (p. 191)	departure (p. 199)
downcast (p. 178)	moored (adj., p. 191)	frauds (p. 199)
*adjoining (p. 179)	floundering (p. 192)	recovery (p. 199)
eddying (adj., p. 184)		*circuitous (p. 199)

Special Glossary

portcullis - a heavy iron grating that can be raised and lowered to serve as a gate

flagons - narrow-necked jugs or bottles

turnkey - a jailer or prison guard

mere - *(archaic)* a pond

kine - *(archaic)* cattle

gammers - old women (from "godmothers")

upholden - variation of "upheld"

DISCUSSION QUESTIONS AND ACTIVITIES

Section I. Read chapters 9 and 10. Discuss your responses to the questions and activities with a classmate. Then write your answers independently.

1. **What useful information does Bilbo learn from wandering around in the Elvenking's palace? How does he use this information to help the dwarves?**

_____

_____

_____

_____

_____

_____

_____

2. **What is Bilbo's escape plan? What problems does he encounter? What is the final result?**

_____

_____

_____

_____

_____

_____

3. **What is unusual about the Lake-town? Using the graphic organizer below, list information given about both the past history and present situation of Lake-town. (Note: you may find it helpful to reread the explanation Thorin gave Bilbo near the end of chapter 1 concerning the history of the Mountain, the dwarves, and the human beings who were their neighbors.)**

Lake-town in the Past	Lake-town in the Present

4. **How does the Master of Lake-town really feel about the dwarves and their mission? Why does he pretend to welcome them? What are his main concerns?**

5. **By the end of chapter 10, the dwarves are no longer the only ones interested in the treasure under the Mountain. What other parties are now aware of the treasure and hoping for a share in it? How do you think this situation might affect the results of the dwarves' quest?**

_____

_____

_____

_____

_____

_____

_____

Make A
Prediction:

How will Bilbo and the dwarves reach the Lonely Mountain without being observed by the dragon? What will they find when they arrive?

Vocabulary List B

bleak (p. 202)
desolation (p. 202)
waning (n., p. 202)
exposed (adj., p. 202)
ledge (p. 204)
mishap (p. 205)
crannies (p. 206)
brooded (p. 206)
aimlessly (p. 206)
enclosure (p. 207)
roving (p. 208)
vapor (p. 209)
debated (p. 210)
exceeding (p. 210)
calculating (adj., p. 211)
*treacherous (p. 211)
ruddy (p. 213)

pierced (p. 214)
dire (p. 214)
menace (n., p. 214)
cowered (p. 215)
*insignificant (p. 215)
wrath (p. 217)
smoldering (adj., p. 218)
sufficiently (p. 218)
perplexed (p. 218)
extent (p. 218)
wily (p. 219)
lore (p. 220)
utterly (p. 220)
calamities (p. 220)
creditable (p. 221)
scoffed (p. 221)
skulking (p. 222)
unaccountable (p. 222)

grievous (p. 222)
cartage (p. 223)
unassessably (p. 223)
*devastating (p. 224)
gloated (p. 224)
antiquated (p. 224)
impenetrable (p. 224)
flawless (p. 225)
staggering (adj., p. 225)
detain (p. 225)
*dubious (p. 227)
stratagems (p. 227)
*foreboding (n., p. 227)
lure (v., p. 228)
in earnest (p. 228)
marrow (p. 229)
avalanche (p. 230)

Special Glossary

spur - a ridge sticking out from the base of a mountain

rent - a tear

The Writer's Craft

Dialogue and *Riddles*

A **dialogue** in literature is a conversation between two characters. Dialogues are often found at critical points in the plot. Two important dialogues found in earlier chapters of *The Hobbit* are the dialogue between Bilbo and Gandalf in chapter 1, and the dialogue between Bilbo and Gollum in chapter 5. The dialogue between Bilbo and Gollum contains examples of a very old form of literature: the **riddle.** Riddles, which are guessing games often based on words with double meanings, have existed for many centuries in almost every language. Bilbo's riddle game with Gollum in chapter 5 was a formal one, where the rules and rewards were clearly stated. In another important dialogue found in chapter 12, Bilbo speaks in riddles that are implied rather than explicit. Who is Bilbo's opponent this time? What are the rewards of this riddle game?

DISCUSSION QUESTIONS AND ACTIVITIES

Section II. Read chapters 11 and 12. Discuss your responses to the questions and activities with a classmate. Then write your answers independently.

1. **Describe the Lonely Mountain. What signs do the travelers see of the dragon's presence there?**

2. **The travelers left Lake-town filled with enthusiasm and excitement, and chapter 10 ends with the sentence, "The only person thoroughly unhappy was Bilbo." How has the situation changed by the time they reach the Mountain? Why is Bilbo excited when he sees the setting sun and the new crescent moon in the sky at the same time? (Hint: you might want to reread the last pages of chapter 3.)**

_____

_____

_____

_____

_____

_____

3. **Why do you think the narrator says that going on down the tunnel into the heart of the Mountain was "the bravest thing [Bilbo] ever did"? What does he find at the end of it? Why do you think Bilbo takes the golden cup back with him to the tunnel's entrance?**

_____

_____

_____

_____

_____

_____

4. **When the dwarves first see the golden cup, they are very pleased. Why does their position change to anger afterwards? How has Bilbo's status among them changed? What does he propose to do next?**

_____

_____

_____

_____

_____

_____

_____

5. **In one column of the chart below, list useful information the dragon acquires from his dialogue with Bilbo, as well as questions that continue to puzzle him. In the other column, list useful information that Bilbo acquires at this time, and things that still worry him.**

	Smaug	**Bilbo**
Useful information acquired		
Worries and concerns		

Make A
Prediction:

**What will happen
when Smaug attacks
the Lake-town?
Will Bilbo and the
dwarves find another
way out of the Moun-
tain?**

Literature-Related Writing

1. Write an **article** for the *Lake-town Reporter* on the arrival of the dwarves. You may wish to include excerpts from interviews with the Master, the raft-elves, the captain of the guards, and/or one of the dwarves.

2. Pretend you are Bilbo. Write a **journal entry** describing your feelings after your meeting with Smaug.

3. Continue to work on the **fantasy story** you began earlier. Include a **dialogue** between two major characters. Do not finish your story yet.

Extension Activities

1. Make a map showing Lake-town, the Mountain, and the settings of the various incidents recounted in this section. You may refer to the maps found in the front of your book, but you should not copy them directly, since neither one fully meets the requirements of this activity.

2. Draw or paint a picture illustrating a scene from this section.

3. Make a diagram of a cross-section of the Mountain, showing the secret door, tunnel, treasure hoard, and Main Gate.

Discussion Guide #5

Chapters 13–19

Vocabulary List A

pallid (p. 235)
tinged (p. 235)
caressing (p. 237)
adornments (p. 239)
moldered (p. 239)
befouled (p. 239)
slithered (p. 240)
sobered (p. 242)
sustaining (adj., p. 242)
dominion (p. 243)
*perpetually (p. 243)
marauding (adj., p. 245)
hotfoot (p. 246)
unquenchable (p. 247)
gilded (adj., p. 248)
wither (p. 248)

baiting (n., p. 248)
throes (p. 249)
waxing (adj., p. 249)
mournful (p. 250)
endured (p. 250)
valor (p. 250)
*eminent (p. 251)
benefactors (p. 251)
deposed (p. 251)
aroused (p. 251)
*obtained (p. 251)
ample (p. 251)
*recompense (p. 251)
fabled (adj., p. 252)
contrived (p. 252)
tidings (p. 253)
wheeling (p. 255)

unceasingly (p. 255)
carrion (p. 255)
coveted (p. 256)
decrepit (p. 256)
caper (v., p 257)
spoil (n., p. 257)
amends (n., p. 257)
remnant (p. 257)
*foremost (p. 260)
fragrance (p. 260)
parley (p. 262)
undesigned (p. 263)
lust (n., p. 263)
succored (p. 264)
besieged (adj., p. 265)
truce (p. 265)

 The Writer's Craft

More on *Complications*

You probably remember that **complications** are new problems that the characters have to face. Sometimes complications arise just as the main conflict seems to be solved. Up to this point, the travelers' main conflict was with the forces of evil, particularly the evil dragon Smaug. If the dwarves can find a way to overcome Smaug, their problems will probably be solved. Or will they? What do you think?

DISCUSSION QUESTIONS AND ACTIVITIES

Section I. Read chapters 13 through 15. Discuss your responses to the questions and activities with a classmate. Then write your answers independently.

1. **How do we know that Bilbo is uneasy about taking the Arkenstone? What excuses might he give? Do you think these are good excuses? Why or why not?**

_____

_____

_____

_____

_____

_____

_____

2. **Describe Bard, the "grim-faced man." What is his role in protecting the town from Smaug? Why does the Master of the town fear him?**

_____

_____

_____

_____

_____

_____

_____

_____

3. **What are the consequences of Smaug's attack on the town? What help do the townspeople receive in their great trouble?**

_____

_____

_____

_____

_____

_____

_____

4. **What information does the old raven bring to the dwarves? What advice does he give them? How does Thorin respond?**

_____

_____

_____

_____

_____

_____

_____

5. **On one side of the T-chart below, list Bard's arguments asking the dwarves to share the treasure with the people of Lake-town. On the other side, list Thorin's arguments in reply. What is Bard's final request, and how does Thorin answer him?**

Bard's Arguments for the Dwarves' Sharing the Treasure	Thorin's Arguments for Not Sharing the Treasure

Make A Prediction:

Will the dwarves change their minds and agree to the Lake-people's demands?
What will happen if they do not?

Vocabulary List B

sentinels (p. 269)
comely (p. 271)
heirloom (p. 274)
literally (p. 275)
forbear (p. 275)
redeem (p. 275)
*withhold (p. 276)
hasty (p. 276)
tarry (p. 278)
*reconciliation (p. 278)
rekindled (p. 279)
multitude (p. 281)
vanguard (p. 281)

feint (n., p. 281)
*heedless (p. 282)
ravening (p. 282)
wielded (p. 283)
*restrain (p. 283)
onset (p. 283)
flanks (p. 283)
hemmed (p. 283)
vile (p. 284)
mustering (p. 289)
fray (n., p. 289)
redoubled (p. 289)
fugitives (p. 290)

pursuit (p. 290)
abode (n., p. 291)
strode (p. 292)
moreover (p. 292)
whither (p. 296)
necromancer (p. 297)
banished (p. 297)
esquire (p. 301)
presumed (p. 301)
*extravagant (p. 302)
memoirs (p. 320)
extensive (p. 302)
deserted (p. 303)

Glossary of Special Terms

casket - here, a small box or chest

in league - united for a common goal; allied

hauberk - a medieval coat of armor, usually made of chain mail

mattock - a tool or weapon shaped like a pickax with a flat, sharp blade (or blades)

scimitar - a short, sharp curved sword

helm - *(archaic)* another word for "helmet"

 The Writer's Craft

Climax and *Denouement*

The **climax** of a story is the turning point that leads to a resolution of the main conflict. What is the unexpected climax of *The Hobbit*? How does this crisis lead to resolution of the conflict between the dwarves, men, and elves?

The word **denouement** (day-noo-MANH) refers to the resolution of the conflict: the unraveling of the tangled knots and complications, the "falling into place" of the different bits of the story after the climax. What "loose ends" aresorted out in the denouement of Bilbo's story? Are there hints of conflicts that are still not resolved?

DISCUSSION QUESTIONS AND ACTIVITIES

Section II. Read chapters 16 through 19. Discuss your responses to the questions and activities with a classmate. Then write your answers independently.

1. **What does Bilbo decide to do with the Arkenstone, and why? Why do the Elvenking and Gandalf express admiration for his decision?**

_____

_____

_____

_____

_____

_____

2. **Does Bilbo succeed in preventing war between the dwarves and their opponents? Why or why not?**

_____

_____

_____

_____

_____

_____

3. **What is the *climax* or crisis of the story? How does it lead to a resolution of the conflict? What finally turns the battle in favor of the protagonists (heroes)?**

_____

_____

_____

_____

_____

_____

4. **Describe Thorin's conduct during the final battle. How does his last farewell to Bilbo show his change of heart?**

_____

_____

_____

_____

_____

_____

5. **After the great battle, what change do we observe in the attitude of men, elves, and dwarves toward the treasure? How has Bilbo's "adventure" changed life for the better for the inhabitants of Middle-earth? What evils still threaten their wellbeing?**

_____

_____

_____

_____

_____

_____

 Literature-Related Writing

1. Write a **poem** or **song** (an **ode** or **ballad**) about some of the events recounted in these chapters, such as the devastation of the town, the death of Smaug, Bilbo's attempt at peacemaking, the great battle, and/or the death of Thorin. The poem does not have to contain rhyme.

2. What lessons do you think *The Hobbit* contains that could be applied to conflicts in our modern world? Write a **personal reflection** of at least one page, comparing the quarrels between dwarves, men, and elves to a specific modern-day conflict that you are aware of. Offer constructive suggestions for solving the conflict based on what you have learned.

3. Finish the **fantasy** story you have been writing. Bring the conflict to a **climax** and provide a satisfying **denouement** for your readers.

 Extension Activities

1. Make a map showing the events of the final battle, or make a map of Bilbo's return home with Gandalf.

2. Draw or paint an illustration of a scene from this section of the book.

3. Create a board game based on the adventures and events recounted in *The Hobbit*.

ABOUT THE AUTHOR

John Ronald Reuel Tolkien was born on January 3, 1892, in Bloemfontein, South Africa. His father passed away in 1896 and Tolkien, along with his mother and younger brother, moved back to his mother's home in England, where he was deeply impressed by the contrast between the beautiful countryside and the grim industrial towns and cities. In 1904 Tolkien's mother also passed away. In 1916, after his studies at Oxford University, Tolkien married and went off to France to fight in the trenches of World War I. After the war he taught Anglo-Saxon and English Language and Literature at Oxford University.

Tolkien had been making up invented languages and fanciful stories since his teenage years, and he began to tell them to his four children. He finally submitted *The Hobbit* to a publisher, who accepted it on the recommendation of his ten-year-old son. When it came out in 1937 the book was instantly popular, and Tolkien was asked to write a sequel, which eventually became the *Lord of the Rings* trilogy. Tolkien also published many other works before his death in 1973.

SO, YOU WANT TO READ MORE

If you enjoyed reading *The Hobbit*, you might enjoy reading other tales of fantasy, such as Lloyd Alexander's *The Book of Three, The Black Cauldron, The High King*, and other books in the *Prydain Chronicles*; or C.S. Lewis' *The Lion, the Witch, and the Wardrobe* and other books in the *Chronicles of Narnia* series.

Made in the USA
San Bernardino, CA
19 July 2016